LOW-CALORIE COOKING

Marshall Cavendish

Editor Mary Devine
Designer Graham Beehag

Published by Marshall Cavendish Books Limited
58 Old Compton Street
London W1V 5PA

Printed in Italy by New Interlitho SpA

ISBN 0 86307 379 4

INTRODUCTION

If you are trying to lose weight and lettuce leaves for lunch followed by cottage cheese for dinner sounds depressingly familiar, then it's time for a complete change. Whether cooking for yourself, preparing meals for the family or entertaining friends, it's perfectly possible to serve nutritious, tasty, beautifully presented dishes while *still* keeping to your calorie allowance. All the recipes have been specially selected with weight watchers in mind, so that you can help yourself to three or more satisfying courses every day of the week and say goodbye to dull mealtimes forever.

Our delicious soups and snacks are ideal for lunches and light evening meals, or serve them as the first course at dinner parties. Then choose something special from the main course selection. Many of our recipes use low-fat fish and chicken, but we have also included lamb chops, bacon kebabs and a hearty casserole, because *everyone* likes a change now and then, even slimmers!

For a light accompaniment to the main course, or as a meal in itself, serve one of our deliciously different salads: there are lots of mouthwatering varieties with something to please everyone, and most of the ingredients are available all year round. At the end of an enjoyable meal, most people appreciate an attractively served dessert. However, if treacle tarts and roly poly puddings are on your dieting 'blacklist', then it's probably best to keep them there. But this doesn't mean that you have to deny yourself delectable desserts forever – just take a look at our marvellously light selection; the calorie counts are so low that you can afford to indulge yourself every day if you like! Most of the recipes are fruit-based and avoid the usual pitfalls such as thick cream, which your family and dinner guests might love, but which *you* can avoid by substituting low-fat yoghurt.

All the recipes in *Low-Calorie Cooking* are easy to follow and the delightful colour photographs show you just how good the finished dish will look. A handy panel of Cook's Notes accompanies each recipe giving plenty of useful advice on buying and preparing, timing and serving, plus of course, calorie counts.
It makes sense to keep to a healthy, well-balanced diet, and your body will thank you for it in years to come, so why not start now by choosing from the tempting selection of delicious recipes in *Low-Calorie Cooking*?

CONTENTS

STARTERS & SNACKS

MAIN COURSES

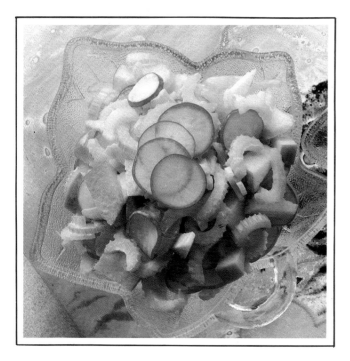

SALADS

DESSERTS

STARTERS & SNACKS

Chilled pea and bean soup

SERVES 4

750 g/1½ lb peas, shelled, and 6 of
   the best pods reserved (see
   Cook's tip)
500 g/1 lb broad beans, shelled
25 g/1 oz margarine or butter
1 large onion, finely chopped
850 ml/1½ pints chicken stock
1 sprig fresh mint
salt and freshly ground black pepper
150 ml/¼ pint natural yoghurt
¼ teaspoon curry paste
1 clove garlic, crushed (optional)
4 small mint sprigs, to garnish

1 Melt the margarine in a frying-
pan. Add the onion and fry gently
for 5 minutes until soft and lightly
coloured.

2 Pour in the stock and bring to the
boil, then add the peas, reserved
pods, beans, mint sprig and salt and
pepper to taste. Lower the heat,
cover and simmer for 20 minutes.

3 Remove the pods and mint sprig,
leave the soup to cool slightly, then
work in a blender or food processor
until smooth. Or work through the
medium blade of a vegetable mill.
Leave until completely cold.

4 Mix the yoghurt in a bowl with
the curry paste and garlic, if using,
then beat in about 6 tablespoons of
the soup until smooth. Stir the
yoghurt mixture into the soup,
making sure that it is well mixed in.
Refrigerate for at least 30 minutes.

5 To serve: pour the soup into 4
chilled individual soup bowls and
float a mint sprig on top of each.

Cook's Notes

TIME
Preparation and cook-
ing take 70 minutes, but
allow extra time for cooling and
chilling.

VARIATIONS
Frozen peas and beans
may be used. In this
case, you will need 350 g/12 oz
peas and 225 g/8 oz beans. Do
not defrost them before
cooking.

To serve the soup hot, make
up to the end of stage 3, but do
not cool. Pour into a saucepan,
heat gently without boiling,
then stir in the yoghurt mixture.
Garnish with chopped mint.

FREEZING
Pour the cooled soup in
to a rigid container,
seal, label and freeze for 6-8
weeks. To serve: defrost for 6-8
hours in the refrigerator,
stirring occasionally. If too
thick, stir in a little cold milk.

COOK'S TIP
Pea pods have a
deliciously strong pea
taste. They are too fibrous and
stringy to be included in a soup,
but if added during the first part
of cooking and then removed,
they will add extra flavour.

● 150 calories/625 kj per portion

Tomato rice soup

SERVES 4

500 g/1 lb fresh tomatoes, chopped
400 g/14 oz can tomatoes
1 tablespoon tomato purée
150 ml/¼ pint water
salt and freshly ground black pepper
50 g/2 oz long-grain rice
2 tablespoons medium sherry
  (optional, see Variation)
1 tablespoon finely chopped
  parsley, to garnish

1 Put all the ingredients except the rice, sherry, if using, and parsley into a large saucepan. Bring to the boil, stirring, then lower the heat, cover and simmer for 30 minutes.
2 Pass the contents of the saucepan through a sieve, or leave to cool slightly, then purée in a blender and sieve (see Cook's tip).
3 Pour the sieved tomato purée back into the rinsed-out pan and bring back to the boil. Stir in the rice, lower the heat, cover and simmer for about 15 minutes or until the rice is tender.
4 Stir in the sherry, if using, taste and adjust seasoning, then pour into warmed individual soup bowls. Sprinkle with parsley and serve at once.

Cook's Notes

TIME
Preparation and cooking take about 1 hour.

VARIATION
Use 2 tablespoons single cream instead of the sherry, and swirl a little into each bowl just before sprinkling with parsley.

SERVING IDEAS
Serve with hot whole-meal rolls.

COOK'S TIP
It is essential to sieve the tomato mixture, to remove the pips and skins.

●80 calories/325 kj per portion

Curried turnip soup

SERVES 4

500 g/1 lb small turnips, quartered (see Cook's tip)

salt

25 g/1 oz margarine or butter

1 small onion, finely chopped

2 teaspoons mild curry powder (see Variation)

600 ml/1 pint chicken stock

1 teaspoon sugar

juice of ½ lemon

freshly ground black pepper

150 ml/¼ pint single cream

1 tablespoon finely chopped parsley, to garnish

1 Blanch the turnips by plunging them into a large pan of boiling salted water and simmering for 3 minutes. Drain at once.

2 Melt the margarine in a large saucepan and add the turnips with the onion. Cover the pan and cook for 5 minutes over very gentle heat, shaking the pan occasionally to prevent the vegetables from sticking.

3 Stir in the curry powder, then pour in the stock. Add the sugar and lemon juice and season to taste with salt and pepper. Cover the pan and simmer over low heat for about 10 minutes or until the turnips are soft.

4 Press the turnips and liquid through a sieve, or leave to cool then purée in a blender.

5 Return the turnip purée to the rinsed-out pan and heat through thoroughly. Taste and adjust seasoning then pour immediately into warmed individual soup bowls. Swirl cream into each portion and sprinkle with parsley.

Gingered aubergine dip

SERVES 4

1 kg/2 lb firm aubergines, stems
   removed
175 ml/6 fl oz natural yoghurt
1 clove garlic, crushed (optional)
1 tablespoon light soft brown sugar
1 teaspoon grated fresh root
   ginger
½ teaspoon cumin powder
salt and freshly ground black pepper
fresh coriander or parsley sprigs, to
   garnish (optional)

1 Heat the oven to 200C/400F/Gas 6.
Prick the aubergines all over with a
fork, then put them into a roasting
tin and bake in the oven for 45-60
minutes, until they feel really soft
when they are pressed with the
back of a spoon.

Cook's Notes

TIME
Preparing and cooking
1¼ hours, plus chilling.

SERVING IDEAS
Serve the dip with small
pieces of toasted pitta
bread and raw vegetables, such
as carrot and cucumber sticks,
strips of red and green pepper,
tomato wedges, lengths of
celery and cauliflower florets.

●65 calories/275 kj per portion

PREPARATION
To extract the aubergine
juices:

*Hold the halved aubergines over a
dish and squeeze gently in your
hand so that the juices run out.*

2 Remove the aubergines from the
oven and leave until cool enough to
handle. Cut them in half lengthways, and squeeze gently in your
hand to drain off the bitter juices
(see Preparation). Scoop out flesh
and leave until cold.
3 Put aubergine flesh in a blender
with the yoghurt, the garlic, if
using, sugar, ginger, cumin and salt
and pepper to taste. Blend until
smooth. Transfer to 1 large or 4
small serving dishes. Refrigerate for
2-3 hours to allow dip to firm up.
4 Just before serving, garnish with
coriander or parsley sprigs, if liked.

Butter bean dip with crudités

SERVES 4

100 g/4 oz dried butter beans, soaked in cold water overnight (see Cook's tips)
4-6 tablespoons good-quality olive oil
1 tablespoon red wine vinegar
1 clove garlic, crushed (optional)
salt and freshly ground black pepper

CRUDITES
1 small cauliflower, broken into florets
1 cucumber, cut into sticks
2 celery stalks, cut into sticks
2 carrots, cut into sticks
1 small green pepper, deseeded and cut into strips
1 small red pepper, deseeded and cut into strips
bunch of radishes

1 Drain the beans and rinse thoroughly under cold running water. Put them in a large saucepan, cover with fresh cold water and bring to the boil. Lower the heat, half cover with a lid and simmer for about 1¼ hours or until the beans are tender. Add more water to the pan during the cooking time if necessary.

2 Drain the beans, reserving the cooking liquid. Put the beans in a blender with 4 tablespoons oil, the vinegar, garlic, if using, a little salt and pepper and 4 tablespoons of the reserved cooking liquid. Blend until thick and smooth, adding a little more liquid if the mixture is too thick.

3 Taste and adjust seasoning, then spoon the mixture into a small bowl and fork over the top; or heap the mixture up in the centre of a large flat serving plate.

4 Serve the crudités in a shallow basket or salad bowl, or stand the bowl of dip in the centre of a large plate and arrange the crudités around the edge of the plate. If you like, drizzle 2 tablespoons oil over the top of the dip just before serving (see Did you know). Serve at room temperature or refrigerate for about 1 hour before serving and serve chilled.

 TIME
Cooking the dried beans takes 1¼ hours and preparing the dip then takes 30 minutes.

 COOK'S TIPS
If you do not have time to soak the beans in cold water overnight, you can cut down the soaking time considerably by using hot water. Put the beans in a large saucepan, cover with cold water and bring to the boil. Drain and repeat, then remove from the heat and leave to soak in the hot water for 2 hours.

To save even more time, you could use a 425 g/15 oz can butter beans, which are pre-cooked. The whole dip can then be made within 30 minutes.

PRESSURE COOKING
Dried butter beans can be cooked in a pressure cooker. Soak and rinse as in recipe, then cook at high (H) pressure for 20 minutes.

 SERVING IDEAS
The butter bean dip makes a filling salad meal for 4, or a starter for 8.

 FREEZING
The dip freezes well, either in the dish from which it will be served or in a rigid container. Store for up to 3 months and allow 2 hours for defrosting at room temperature before serving.

 DID YOU KNOW
Finishing off the dip with extra oil drizzled on top is usual in Middle Eastern countries, where dips and pâtés made from pulses are very popular. If you do not like too oily a taste, this can be easily omitted.

●225 calories/950 kj per portion

10

Egg and lettuce pinwheels

MAKES ABOUT 20

5 large crisp lettuce leaves (see Buying guide)
3 hard-boiled eggs, roughly chopped
about 25 g/1 oz margarine or butter, softened
25 g/1 oz Danish Blue cheese, crumbled

1 Cut off a thin slice from the stalk end of each lettuce leaf to remove the thickest part of the stalk. Wash and gently pat dry on absorbent paper. Set aside.
2 Make the filling: put the eggs into a bowl with 25 g/1 oz margarine and the cheese. Mash with a fork to form a smooth paste, adding a little more margarine if the mixture is too stiff to blend.
3 Place 1 lettuce leaf on a work surface and spoon 1 tablespoon of the egg mixture into the centre. Gently spread the mixture over the lettuce leaf right up to the edges. Starting at the trimmed end, tightly roll up the leaf to enclose the egg mixture. Wrap firmly in cling film immediately after rolling.
4 Spread, roll and wrap the remaining lettuce leaves in the same way and refrigerate overnight.
5 To serve: unwrap the rolls and cut with a sharp knife into 2.5 cm/ 1 inch lengths. Serve at once.

Cook's Notes

 TIME
About 20 minutes preparation, plus overnight chilling.

 BUYING GUIDE
Choose a cos, Webb's Wonder or iceberg lettuce for this recipe.

VARIATIONS
For a milder flavour, use full-fat soft cheese instead of blue cheese and season with salt and pepper and a little sweet paprika.
Alternatively, replace the blue cheese with anchovy paste, available in tubes and jars from delicatessens and large supermarkets.

 SERVING IDEAS
Serve as a summery starter, garnished with tomato wedges and cucumber slices. These pinwheels also make delicate accompaniments for cocktails – arrange attractively on a serving platter and garnish with tomato or sprigs of watercress and parsley for a pretty effect.

●25 calories/100 kj per roll

Spinach and carrot layer loaf

SERVES 4-6

750 g/1½ lb spinach, stalks and large midribs removed (see Buying guide)
750 g/1½ lb carrots, grated
salt
freshly grated nutmeg
1 teaspoon finely grated orange zest
freshly ground black pepper
50 g/2 oz margarine or butter
margarine, for greasing
orange slices and parsley sprigs, to garnish

1 Heat the oven to 180C/350F/Gas 4 and grease a 500 g/1 lb loaf tin.
2 Put the spinach into a large saucepan with only the water that clings to leaves after washing. Sprinkle with salt, cover and cook over low heat for 5 minutes, shaking the pan constantly until very soft.
3 Drain the spinach thoroughly and squeeze with your hand to remove as much water as possible. Chop finely, season to taste with salt and nutmeg, then set aside.
4 Mix carrots and orange zest together, then season with salt and pepper to taste. Put half in the tin, then cover with the spinach. Arrange the remaining carrots on top of the spinach. Set aside.
5 Heat the margarine in a small saucepan over low heat until melted then pour over carrots in the tin.
6 Bake in the oven for 1 hour. To serve: run a knife around sides of tin, invert a warmed serving plate on top and turn out loaf. Garnish with orange slices and parsley sprigs. Cut into slices and serve at once (see Serving ideas).

Cook's Notes

TIME
Preparation 20 minutes; cooking 1 hour.

VARIATION
Grated celeriac may be used instead of carrots.

BUYING GUIDE
When fresh spinach is unavailable, use 225g/8 oz frozen chopped spinach instead of fresh.

SERVING IDEAS
Serve as a light snack, accompanied by hot, wholemeal rolls and butter. Alternatively, serve loaf as a colourful vegetable accompaniment to either boiled ham or braised beef.
For a more dramatic effect, try drizzling soured cream over the loaf before serving.

● 180 calories/750 kj per portion

Cottage cheese and ham cocottes

SERVES 4

225 g/8 oz cottage cheese
1 tablespoon vegetable oil
1 small onion, finely chopped
100 g/4 oz mushrooms, chopped
2 eggs, lightly beaten
50 g/2 oz ham, diced
pinch of freshly grated nutmeg
salt and freshly ground black pepper
25 g/1 oz butter, melted
parsley sprigs, to garnish

1 Heat the oven to 200C/400F/Gas 6.

2 Heat the oil in a small sauce-pan, add the onion and fry gently until it is soft.
3 Add the mushrooms and fry for 1-2 minutes only, stirring constantly. Remove the saucepan from the heat and cool.
4 Sieve the cottage cheese into a bowl and beat in the beaten eggs, a little at a time.
5 Add the diced ham to the cheese mixture with the onion and mush-rooms. Add the nutmeg, then season to taste with salt and pepper.
6 Brush 4 ramekins or cocottes with the melted butter and divide the mixture between them.
7 Place on a baking sheet and bake for about 20-25 minutes or until well risen, and brown and bubbly on top. Serve immediately, garnished with sprigs of parsley.

Cook's Notes

 TIME
Preparation 10 minutes, baking 25 minutes.

 VARIATION
Replace the ham with 75 g/3 oz peeled prawns and the mushrooms with a small amount of canned or frozen sweetcorn.

●210 calories/875 kj per portion

Chicken and parsley mould

SERVES 4

2 chicken joints, each weighing about 275 g/10 oz
1 small onion, quartered
1 bay leaf
salt and freshly ground black pepper
1 rounded tablespoon (1 sachet) powdered gelatine
3 tablespoons cold water
2 hard-boiled eggs, chopped
40 g/1½ oz finely chopped fresh parsley

1 Rinse out an 850 ml/1½ pint metal mould with cold water, shake off the excess, then refrigerate.
2 Put the chicken in a saucepan with the onion and bay leaf and cover with cold water. Season with salt and pepper and bring to the boil, skimming off any scum as it rises to the surface. Cover and simmer for about 45 minutes or until the chicken is cooked (the juices run clear when chicken is pierced).
3 Strain the cooking liquid and reserve 600 ml/1 pint of this stock.

 TIME
Preparation and cooking time about 1 hour, setting time at least 6 hours or overnight.

 VARIATIONS
To cut down on time you can use ready-cooked chicken and stock made with a cube, but the flavour of the dish will not be so good.

 SERVING IDEAS
Serve as a light lunch or supper dish with brown bread and butter and a salad, or alone as an unusual dinner party starter for 6. Do not refrigerate again before serving—the mould has a better flavour if it is served at room temperature.

●155 calories/650 kj per portion

4 Remove the skin and bones from the chicken, cut the flesh into neat pieces and set aside.
5 Sprinkle the gelatine over the water in a small heatproof bowl and leave to stand for 5 minutes until spongy. Stand bowl in a pan of gently simmering water for 1-2 minutes until the gelatine has dissolved, stirring occasionally. Stir in the reserved stock and salt and pepper to taste.
6 In a bowl, carefully mix the chicken with the hard-boiled eggs and about two-thirds of the parsley.
7 Spoon the chicken mixture into the chilled mould, then pour in enough stock mixture to fill the mould. Add the rest of the parsley to the remaining stock mixture.
8 Refrigerate the mould and the stock for at least 6 hours or overnight until both have set.
9 To serve: ease edges away from the sides of the mould with your fingers. Dip the mould into very hot water for 1-2 seconds then invert a dampened plate on top. Holding mould and plate firmly, invert giving a sharp shake halfway round. Lift off the mould. Chop the jellied stock with a knife. Serve the mould cut into slices with the jelly handed separately in a dish.

Crab-stuffed tomatoes

SERVES 4

8 large tomatoes
275-300 g/10-12 oz canned or frozen
   crabmeat (see Buying guide)
grated zest of 2 lemons
4 teaspoons lemon juice
2 tablespoons thick mayonnaise
4 tablespoons cottage cheese, sieved
2 punnets mustard and cress,
   snipped
salt and freshly ground black pepper
few drops of Tabasco

1 Slice off the top of each tomato and set aside. Using a grapefruit knife or teaspoon, gently scoop out the flesh and seeds, taking care not to pierce the tomato shells (see Economy). Turn them upside down on absorbent paper and leave them to drain while you prepare the crab filling.

2 In a bowl, mix together the crabmeat, lemon zest and juice, mayonnaise and sieved cottage cheese (see Cook's tip). Lightly stir in the mustard and cress and season to taste with salt, pepper and the Tabasco. Cover the bowl and chill the mixture in the refrigerator for 1-2 hours.

3 Spoon the crab mixture into the tomato shells, filling them as full as possible without letting the mixture run down the sides of the tomatoes. Carefully replace the tomato tops on the crab stuffing and serve the tomatoes at once.

Cook's Notes

TIME
Preparation takes 30 minutes. Allow 1-2 hours for chilling the stuffing.

SERVING IDEAS
These stuffed tomatoes are very versatile: they make an unusual starter for a dinner party, or may be served as a main meal with a mixed salad and French bread. For a tasty supper dish, serve the tomatoes on circles of fried or toasted bread, garnished with watercress.

BUYING GUIDE
Canned and frozen crabmeat is sold in varying weights according to individual brands. Exact weight of crabmeat is not critical for this recipe as the size of the tomatoes will vary as well.

ECONOMY
Discard the seeds and use the scooped-out tomato flesh for sandwiches.

COOK'S TIP
If you find the flavour of crab rather strong, use less crabmeat and add more cottage cheese when you are mixing the filling.

VARIATION
Tomatoes may be stuffed with all sorts of mixtures. Substitute drained, mashed tuna fish for the crabmeat in this recipe. Or try mixing equal quantities of cream cheese with sieved cottage cheese and adding some chopped prawns or chopped walnuts. You can also try lime juice instead of lemon juice.

●140 calories/600 kj per portion

Bean-stuffed cabbage leaves

SERVES 4
12 white cabbage leaves
1 tablespoon vegetable oil
1 onion, finely chopped
100 g/4 oz haricot beans, soaked
  overnight (see Buying guide)
600 ml/1 pint chicken stock
salt
1 tablespoon tomato purée
juice of 1 lemon
freshly ground black pepper

1 Heat the oil in a large saucepan, add the onion and fry gently for 5 minutes until soft and lightly coloured. Drain the beans and add them to the pan with the stock. Bring to the boil, then lower the heat slightly and simmer for about 1 hour or until the beans are tender.
2 Meanwhile, bring a pan of salted water to the boil. Remove the tough rib at the base of the cabbage leaves and blanch the leaves, 2 at a time, in the boiling water until pliable. Drain carefully, refresh under cold running water, then lay flat and pat dry with absorbent paper.
3 Drain the beans, then mash them roughly with a wooden spoon. Stir in the tomato purée, half the lemon juice and salt and pepper to taste.
4 Place 1 tablespoon of the bean mixture at the stalk end of 8 cabbage leaves. Fold the 2 sides over the filling, then roll up each cabbage leaf to form a neat parcel.
5 Line a large saucepan with the remaining cabbage leaves and tightly pack the cabbage rolls into the pan, join side down. Pour over the remaining lemon juice and enough cold water to cover. Sprinkle with salt, then place a small plate on top of leaves to keep them in place.
6 Bring to the boil, cover the pan, then lower the heat slightly and simmer gently for 1 hour.
7 Remove the plate and transfer the rolls to a warmed serving platter with a slotted spoon. Serve at once.

Cook's Notes

TIME
Cooking the beans takes about 1 hour. Assembling and cooking the stuffed leaves takes 1½ hours.

SERVING IDEAS
These stuffed cabbage leaves are a delicious accompaniment to pork and bacon dishes. They also make a substantial supper if served with turmeric rice.

BUYING GUIDE
Buy the beans from a shop with a quick turn-over. Old beans become tough and no amount of cooking softens them properly.

●130 calories/550 kj per portion

Lemon veal

SERVES 4

4 veal escalopes, weighing 100-175 g/
   4-6 oz each (see Preparation)
40 g/1½ oz butter
150 ml/¼ pint chicken stock
finely grated zest of ½ lemon
juice of 1 lemon
2 teaspoons finely chopped fresh
   sage, or 1 teaspoon dried sage
salt and freshly ground black pepper

TO GARNISH
sage sprigs
lemon slices

1 Heat the oven to 110C/225F/Gas ¼.
2 Melt the butter in a large frying-pan until sizzling, add the veal escalopes and fry for 2-3 minutes on each side until pale golden and cooked through.
3 Transfer the veal escalopes to a warmed serving dish and keep warm in the oven. Pour the stock into the pan and add the lemon zest, juice and sage. Bring to the boil, stirring, then lower the heat and simmer for 4-5 minutes until syrupy. Remove from the heat and taste and adjust seasoning.
4 Pour the sauce evenly over the veal escalopes and serve at once, garnished with sage sprigs and lemon slices.

Cook's Notes

TIME
Preparation and cooking take 25 minutes.

PREPARATION
If the escalopes have not already been beaten flat by the butcher, place them between 2 sheets of greaseproof paper and beat them with a wooden mallet or rolling pin to a thickness of 5 mm/¼ inch.

ECONOMY
Pork tenderloin makes a good and less expensive alternative to veal. Turkey escalopes can also be used.

 WATCHPOINTS
Add the escalopes as soon as the butter sizzles, but before it starts to brown.
  Take care not to overcook the escalopes or they will be dry and tough.

 SERVING IDEAS
Serve with peas—try them cooked French-style with onion and shredded lettuce. Buttered new potatoes or noodles are also suitable accompaniments.

●225 calories/950 kj per portion

Chicken escalopes provençal

SERVES 4

4 chicken breasts, each weighing about 175 g/6 oz, skinned
25 g/1 oz plain flour
salt and freshly ground black pepper
2 tablespoons vegetable oil
50 g/2 oz margarine or butter
1-2 cloves garlic, halved
400 g/14 oz can tomatoes
2 spring onions, chopped
2 level teaspoons tomato purée
1/2 green pepper, deseeded and diced
1/2 teaspoon dried oregano
1 tablespoon chopped fresh parsley, to garnish

1 Heat the oven to 110C/225F/Gas 1/4.
2 Place the chicken breasts between 2 sheets of greaseproof paper on a board or work surface. With a wooden rolling pin or mallet, beat the chicken breasts until about 1 cm/ 1/2 inch thick. Pat dry with absorbent paper (see Cook's tips).
3 Spread the flour out on a flat plate and season with salt and pepper. Coat the flattened escalopes on both sides with the seasoned flour.
4 Heat the oil and margarine in a large frying-pan. When the foam subsides, add the garlic and fry for 1 minute, then remove with a slotted spoon (see Cook's tips).
5 Add the escalopes to the pan and fry over moderate heat for 3-5 minutes on each side (see Cook's tips). Remove from pan, drain on absorbent paper. Keep warm in the oven.
6 Pour off most of the fat from the pan. Add the tomatoes, with their juice, and all the remaining ingredients except the parsley. Stir well, bring to the boil, then lower the heat and simmer for 5 minutes. Season to taste with salt and pepper.
7 Return the escalopes to the pan to heat through in the tomato sauce for 5 minutes. Transfer to a warmed serving dish and sprinkle with chopped parsley. Serve at once.

Cook's Notes

TIME
Preparation takes about 20 minutes, cooking about 25 minutes.

COOK'S TIPS
The chicken breasts must be completely dry before coating with flour, as they will not brown if fried when damp.

The garlic is used to flavour the butter for frying the escalopes, then removed, so that the dish is just subtly garlic flavoured.

The fat for frying the escalopes must be sizzling in order to brown them, but not too hot, or they will burn. The escalopes can be fried in 2 batches if necessary.

DID YOU KNOW
Dishes with the name provençal are typical of the Provence region of southern France, and always contain garlic. For real perfection, they should be made with the mild garlic that thrives in the Mediterranean region, not the strong, northern European variety.

● 280 calories/1175 kj per portion

Stir-fry chicken

275g/10 oz boneless raw chicken,
   cut into bite-sized pieces
2 tablespoons soy sauce
1 tablespoon sherry or water
¼ teaspoon ground ginger
2 teaspoons cornflour
2 tablespoons vegetable oil
3 spring onions, trimmed and sliced
1 small green pepper, deseeded and
   diced
100g/4 oz mushrooms, chopped
½ small or ¼ large cauliflower,
   divided into about 10 florets
4 tablespoons water, or chicken
   stock if available
salt
2 tomatoes, sliced

1 In a bowl mix together the soy
sauce, sherry, ginger and cornflour.
Stir in the chicken pieces and coat
evenly in the mixture.
2 Heat 1 tablespoon oil in a large
frying-pan or wok over moderate
heat until very hot, then stir-fry the
meat for 1 minute, turning it constantly. Transfer the meat to a plate
and keep it warm in a low oven.
3 Heat the remaining oil over
moderate heat until very hot. Add
the spring onions, green pepper,
mushrooms and cauliflower and stir-
fry for 1 minute. Add the water or
stock and cook for 2-3 minutes.
4 Return the chicken to the pan.
Season with salt. Stir in the tomatoes
and heat through over moderate
heat for 1 minute. Serve at once.

Cook's Notes

TIME
A quick dish that takes
25 minutes.

COOK'S TIP
For stir-frying the
Chinese use a wok — a
metal pan with sloping sides.
The principle of stir-frying is to
cook quickly over high heat, so
the oil must be hot and the
ingredients small.

● 140 calories/600kj per portion

Barbecued chicken drumsticks

SERVES 4

8 chicken drumsticks
4 tablespoons tomato ketchup
2 tablespoons Worcestershire sauce
½ small onion, finely chopped
25 g/1 oz soft brown sugar
1 tablespoon lemon juice
celery salt
sweet paprika

1 Combine the tomato ketchup with the Worcestershire sauce, onion, sugar and lemon juice. Season with celery salt and paprika to taste. Brush the mixture over the drumsticks. Leave to marinate in a cool place for as long as possible (up to 8 hours, see Cook's tips).
2 Heat the grill to moderate.

Remove the drumsticks from the marinade and cook under the grill for 15-20 minutes until cooked through, turning and basting occasionally with the marinade.
3 Mix the juices in the grill pan with any remaining marinade and spoon over the drumsticks. Serve at once.

Cook's Notes

 TIME
Preparation 5 minutes, and up to 8 hours to marinate. Cooking takes 15-20 minutes.

 SERVING IDEAS
Serve with sautéed sliced aubergines, green or red peppers and tomatoes, accompanied by chopped cucumber with yoghurt and crusty bread.

 VARIATIONS
Chinese-style spare ribs of pork can be cooked in the same way; so, too, can strips of belly pork.

COOK'S TIPS
The flavour is improved if the drumsticks are left to marinate for several hours. The drumsticks can be skinned before marinating if preferred, but the skin does help keep the flesh moist during cooking, and is extra nice if grilled until crisp. In summer, these drumsticks are especially good if cooked on a barbecue.

●275 calories/1150 kj per portion

Pressed tongue

SERVES 8

1 salted ox tongue, weighing about
    2 kg/4½ lb (see Buying guide)
1 onion, thickly sliced
2 carrots, thickly sliced
1 bay leaf
6 whole black peppercorns

1 Put the tongue in a large bowl, cover with cold water and leave to soak for 12 hours or overnight.

2 Drain and weigh the tongue and calculate the cooking time at 30 minutes per 500 g/1 lb. Put the tongue in a large saucepan, cover with fresh cold water, then bring slowly to the boil. Boil for 5 minutes, then drain.

3 Return the tongue to the pan, cover with fresh cold water and add the onion, carrots, bay leaf and peppercorns. Bring slowly to the boil, then lower the heat and simmer very gently for the calculated cooking time until very tender (see Cook's tips).

4 Transfer the tongue carefully to a large bowl and cover with fresh cold water. Leave for about 15 minutes or until cool enough to handle.

5 Place the tongue on a board and,

Cook's Notes

TIME
Allow overnight soaking time, then 5 minutes for pre-boiling. Cooking takes about 2 hours; cooling and skinning about 30 minutes. Allow overnight setting time.

BUYING GUIDE
Ox tongues are considered the best of all tongues for flavour. They are large, weighing between 1.5-3 kg/3-6½ lb. They are sold fresh or salted, but salted tongue has a better flavour.

WATCHPOINTS
The tongue must simmer very gently during the long cooking time; if allowed to boil, it will be tough.

Use strong kitchen tongs and take care to have firm hold of the tongue as it is slippery.

COOK'S TIPS
It is important that the tongue is cooked until very tender. To test: the bones near the root should pull out easily. In the old days, it was said that the flesh should be soft enough to be pierced with a straw.

To ensure the finished tongue has a good shape, it must be set in a tin that will only just hold it, and be well weighted down.

●275 calories/1150 kj per portion

starting at the top, peel off the skin with a sharp knife. Trim off bones and gristle.

6 Turn the tongue on its side, then curl it round into a circle and place in a 18 cm/7 inch cake tin (see Cook's tips).

7 Strain the tongue cooking liquid and pour enough over the tongue so that it comes almost to the edge of the cake tin.

8 Place a small plate that just fits inside the tin on top of the tongue, weight down with a 3.25 kg/7 lb weight and refrigerate overnight, until the tongue is firmly set.

9 Run a knife round the tongue to loosen it from the tin, then dip the base of the tin in hot water for just a few seconds. Invert a serving plate on top of tin. Hold the tin and plate firmly together and invert them, giving a sharp shake halfway round. Lift away the tin.

10 Carve the cold tongue horizontally in thin slices.

Italian fish stew

SERVES 4

4 frozen white fish steaks (cod or
    haddock), each weighing
    150g/5 oz

2 tablespoons olive or vegetable oil
1 onion, finely chopped
1 red pepper, deseeded and
    chopped
2 medium courgettes, chopped
100 g/4 oz mushrooms, quartered if
    large
300 ml/½ pint tomato spaghetti
    sauce (see Buying guide)
1 teaspoon lemon juice
salt and freshly ground black pepper

TO GARNISH
chopped parsley
lemon wedges

1 Heat the grill to moderate.
2 Brush the grill rack with oil, then arrange the frozen fish steaks on the rack in a single layer. Grill for about 15 minutes, turning once ⚠ and brushing the rack with more oil.
3 Meanwhile, heat the remaining oil in a large heavy saucepan. Add the onion, red pepper and courgettes and fry over moderate heat for 10 minutes until softened. Stir in the mushrooms and fry for a further 3 minutes.
4 Stir in the spaghetti sauce and lemon juice. Season to taste with salt and pepper. Cover the saucepan and simmer.
5 When the fish steaks are ready, place them in the pan in a single layer and spoon over the sauce to coat them. Simmer, uncovered, for 5 minutes.
6 Taste and adjust the seasoning. Carefully lift the fish steaks on to a warmed large serving plate and

spoon the sauce over and around them. Sprinkle the fish with chopped parsley and serve the fish stew with lemon wedges.

Cook's Notes

TIME
This dish takes 1 hour to prepare and cook.

WATCHPOINT
Use a fish slice when handling the steaks so that there is less chance of them breaking.

BUYING GUIDE
Tomato spaghetti sauce is available in cans and jars from most supermarkets and delicatessens.

●295 calories/1225 kj per portion

Hearty casserole

SERVES 4

4 lamb hearts, total weight 750 g-
    1 kg/1½-2 lb (see Preparation)
25 g/1 oz margarine or butter
1 large carrot, cut into short, even
    lengths
2 celery stalks, cut into short,
    even lengths
½ green or red pepper, deseeded
    and cut into 5 mm/¼ inch dice
1 large onion, chopped
300 ml/½ pint hot chicken stock
1 bay leaf
salt and freshly ground black pepper
2 tablespoons plain flour
1 tablespoon tomato purée
green or red pepper rings, to
    garnish

1 Pat the hearts dry with absorbent paper and cut across into 1 cm/ ½ inch thick slices.

2 Melt the margarine in a medium saucepan, add the carrot, celery, diced pepper and onion and fry over moderate heat for 5 minutes, stirring frequently. Add the heart slices and fry for a further 2-3 minutes, stirring until the meat is evenly browned.

3 Add the stock to the pan with the bay leaf and salt and pepper to taste. Bring to the boil, stirring, then lower the heat and cover tightly with a lid. Simmer gently for about 1½ hours until the meat is tender. Discard the bay leaf.

4 In a small bowl, blend the flour to a smooth paste with a little cold water. Stir in a little of the hot liquid from the pan, then stir the mixture back into the pan. Bring to the boil, stirring, then simmer for 2-3 minutes until thickened. Stir in the tomato purée, taste and adjust seasoning, then transfer to a warmed serving dish. Garnish with pepper rings and serve piping hot.

Roast chicken with yoghurt

SERVES 4

2 kg/4½ lb oven-ready chicken, skinned, giblets removed

1 clove garlic, crushed with a pinch of salt

2 tablespoons chopped fresh mint

1 tablespoon ground cumin

2 teaspoons sugar

1 teaspoon ground ginger

1 teaspoon salt

½ teaspoon chilli powder

½ teaspoon ground turmeric

½ teaspoon ground mixed spice

3 × 150 g/5 oz cartons natural yoghurt

boiled rice, to serve (optional)

fresh mint, to garnish

1 Wash the chicken and dry thoroughly with absorbent paper. Score it with a very sharp knife, then place the chicken in a large bowl.

2 Mix together the remaining ingredients, reserving 1 carton yoghurt. Pour the mixture over the chicken, cover and leave to marinate in the refrigerator for at least 8 hours, preferably overnight. Spoon the marinade over occasionally.

3 The next day, heat the oven to 190C/375F/Gas 5.

4 Put the chicken into a casserole (see Cook's tip) and pour over the marinade. Cover and roast in the oven for 1½-2 hours or until the chicken is tender and the juices run clear when the flesh is pierced in the thickest part of the thigh with a skewer. Baste occasionally with the marinade during the roasting time.

5 Remove the chicken from the casserole and keep hot. Scrape the juices from the casserole and pour into a heavy-based saucepan. Stir in the remaining yoghurt and heat through gently, whisking constantly and vigorously. ⚠️

6 If serving with boiled rice, spoon it on to a warmed serving dish and place the chicken on top. Pour the yoghurt sauce over and serve at once, garnished with mint.

Cook's Notes

TIME
Preparation 15 minutes, but allow time to marinate for 8 hours or overnight. Cooking time 1½-2 hours.

COOK'S TIP
This is an ideal recipe to use if you have a chicken brick. Soak the brick in cold water for 30 minutes, drain, then put chicken inside. Pour over the marinade, close the brick and put in a cold oven. Heat the oven to 220C/425F/Gas 7 and roast for 1½ hours without opening the oven. Continue from beginning of stage 5.

WATCHPOINT
Do not allow the yoghurt sauce to boil or it will curdle and separate.

● 255 calories/1050 kj per portion

Lemon-grilled herrings

SERVES 4

4 medium herrings, scaled, cleaned and boned (see Preparation)
salt and freshly ground black pepper
juice of 1-1½ lemons
1 teaspoon caraway seeds

1 Rinse the fish and pat them dry. With a sharp knife make 3 diagonal shallow slashes through the skin on one side of each herring.
2 Heat the grill to moderate. Season the herrings inside and out with salt and pepper. Sprinkle the insides with a little lemon juice and lay the herrings, cut side up, on the grill rack. Sprinkle with more lemon juice and half the caraway seeds.
3 Grill the herrings for 10 minutes, turning them over halfway through cooking and sprinkling with the remaining lemon juice and caraway seeds. Transfer to a warmed serving platter and serve at once.

Cook's Notes

TIME
10 minutes preparation, 10 minutes grilling.

PREPARATION
Ask the fishmonger to clean the herrings and remove their heads. You could ask him to bone them for you too, leaving them whole, though not all fishmongers will spare the time to do this, so if possible ask him in advance.

ECONOMY
Ask your fishmonger for the herring roes when he is cleaning the fish. They will make a delicious breakfast or lunch dish for 2. Rinse them lightly and pat dry. Separate the pairs. Roll the roes in flour seasoned with salt and pepper (preferably cayenne), then fry them gently in butter for just 1-2 minutes each side. Serve hot on buttered toast.

VARIATION
Small mackerel could be used instead of herrings.

SERVING IDEAS
Garnish with lemon slices and parsley, and serve with buttered brown bread and salad. These herrings are also good served cold with a crisp green salad.

●185 calories/775 kj per portion

TO BONE HERRINGS

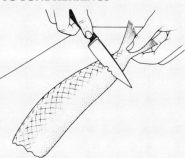

1 *Remove the scales, scraping the fish from tail to head. Cut off fins with scissors.*

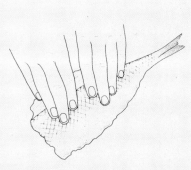

2 *Slit along stomach and open fish out, skin side up. Press to loosen the backbone.*

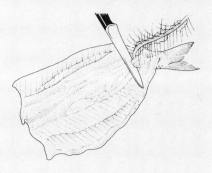

3 *Turn fish over and ease backbone away, starting at head end. Cut it off with the tail.*

Chicken paprikash

SERVES 4

 4 chicken pieces, skinned
15 g/½ oz margarine or butter
 500 g/1 lb onions, finely chopped
1 clove garlic, crushed (optional)
 1 tablespoon sweet paprika
salt and freshly ground black pepper
about 150 ml/¼ pint hot chicken
   stock
150 ml/¼ pint soured cream
snipped chives, to garnish

1 Heat the oven to 180C/350F/Gas 4.
2 Melt the margarine in a large, shallow flameproof casserole big enough to take the chicken pieces in a single layer (see Cook's tip). Add onions and garlic, if using, cover and fry gently for about 45 minutes until a soft, golden brown purée is formed.
3 Raise the heat slightly, then sprinkle in the paprika and salt and pepper to taste. Add the chicken

and spoon over the onion mixture.
4 Cover the casserole and bake in the oven for 45 minutes or until the juices run clear when the thickest part of the chicken flesh is pierced with a skewer. Check the casserole contents regularly and add a little stock from time to time if the chicken appears to be becoming a little too dry. ! *
5 Heat the soured cream in a pan; do not boil, or it will curdle. Pour over the chicken; sprinkle with chives and serve at once.

Chinese-style fish

SERVES 4

1 kg/2 lb red trout, cleaned and
   scaled, with head and tail left on
   (see Buying guide)
salt and freshly ground black pepper
1 tablespoon vegetable oil
1 bunch spring onions, halved
   lengthways and cut into
   2.5 cm/1 inch pieces
1 small piece fresh root ginger,
   finely shredded, or good pinch
   of ground ginger (optional)
1 small green pepper, deseeded
   and finely sliced
100 g/4 oz button mushrooms, very
   thinly sliced
2 tablespoons light soy sauce
2 tablespoons dry sherry
spring onions, to garnish
vegetable oil, for greasing

1 Heat the oven to 180C/350F/Gas 4.
Cut a piece of foil large enough to
contain the fish. Grease with oil.
2 Pat the fish dry inside and out
with absorbent paper and season
with salt and pepper. Place on foil.

3 Heat the oil in a frying-pan, add
the spring onions, ginger if using,
green pepper and mushrooms and
fry briskly for 1 minute, stirring
constantly. Stir in the soy sauce and
sherry and cook for 1 further minute, stirring once or twice.
4 Spread the mixture evenly over
the fish, then seal the foil edges
securely to make a neat parcel.

5 Place on a baking sheet and bake
in the oven for 45 minutes or until
the fish is cooked (the flesh flakes
easily when pierced with the point
of a sharp knife).
6 Carefully remove the trout to a
warmed serving dish. Garnish the
dish with spring onions and spoon
the mushrooms and juices along-
side. Serve at once.

Cook's Notes

TIME
Preparation takes about
15 minutes, cooking
about 45 minutes.

BUYING GUIDE
Red trout, which are
larger than rainbow
trout, are specially bred in trout
farms throughout the year for
their red flesh which turns an
attractive pink when cooked.
Red trout, which represent excellent value for money, are
available filleted from supermarkets: whole fish are sold
only by fishmongers. Other
whole large fish suitable for this
recipe are bream and mullet.

SERVING IDEAS
Serve with Chinese
noodles and a salad of
shredded Chinese leaves.

VARIATION
Transfer the fish to a
warmed serving dish,
carefully reserving the juices in
the foil. Pour the juices into a
small saucepan, add 3 tablespoons fresh orange juice and
1 tablespoon tomato purée and
heat through until bubbling,
stirring constantly. Pour over
the prepared fish, then garnish
and serve as above.

●240 calories/1000 kj per portion

Cod with orange yoghurt sauce

SERVES 4

4 cod steaks, weighing about 175 g/
   6 oz each
3 large oranges
1 tablespoon olive oil
150 g/5 oz natural yoghurt
salt and freshly ground black pepper
15 g/½ oz margarine or butter,
   softened
15 g/½ oz plain flour
2 tablespoons chopped fresh
   parsley

1 Squeeze the juice from 2 of the oranges and mix in a bowl with the olive oil and yoghurt to blend.

2 Season both sides of the cod steaks generously with salt and pepper and place them in an ovenproof dish. Pour the orange and yoghurt mixture evenly over the cod steaks and leave to marinate in a cool place for about 1 hour.

3 Heat the oven to 180C/350F/Gas 4.

4 Cook the cod steaks in the orange and yoghurt mixture in the oven for 20 minutes until the flesh flakes easily when pierced with a knife.

5 While the fish is cooking, peel the remaining orange with a sharp, serrated knife, removing all the pith. Cut the orange into segments, discarding all the membrane.

6 When the fish is cooked, lift it on to a warmed serving platter with a fish slice and keep warm in the oven turned down to 110C/225F/Gas ¼.

7 Pour the orange and yoghurt mixture from the dish into a saucepan. In a small bowl, mash together the margarine and flour until thoroughly blended.

8 Place the saucepan over moderate heat and whisk in the margarine and flour mixture a little at a time until the sauce is smooth (see Cook's tip). Bring the sauce gradually to the boil, and simmer gently for 3-4 minutes. Stir in parsley. Taste and adjust seasoning if necessary.

9 Pour a little sauce over the cod steaks and garnish with the orange segments. Serve at once, handing the remaining sauce separately.

Bacon and cabbage casserole

SERVES 4

4 bacon steaks (each weighing about 100 g/4 oz), cut into 1 cm/½ inch strips (see Buying guide)
40 g/1½ oz margarine or butter
500 g/1 lb cooking apples, peeled, cored and cut into chunks
3 tablespoons white wine or chicken stock
500-750 g/1-1½ lb white cabbage, shredded
1-2 teaspoons caraway seeds (see Did you know)
150 g/5 oz natural yoghurt
freshly ground black pepper

1 Heat the oven to 180C/350F/Gas 4.
2 Melt half the margarine in a large frying-pan, add the bacon strips and apples and cook gently, stirring from time to time, for 5-10 minutes until the apples are soft and beginning to turn pulpy. Add the wine and boil for 1-2 minutes.
3 Meanwhile, melt the remaining margarine in a saucepan and add the cabbage. Stir until the cabbage is coated, then cover the pan and cook gently for about 5 minutes. Shake the pan from time to time to prevent the cabbage from sticking.
4 Remove the saucepan from the heat and add the caraway seeds and yoghurt to the cabbage, stirring well to mix. Season with pepper (see Cook's tip).
5 Turn half the cabbage mixture into a casserole. Spoon the bacon and apple mixture on top and then top with the remaining cabbage mixture. Cover the casserole and cook in the oven for about 30 minutes. Serve hot, straight from the casserole, tossing the bacon and cabbage together.

29

Mustardy lamb chops

SERVES 4

 4 large or 8 small lamb loin chops, trimmed of excess fat
salt and freshly ground black pepper
 fresh parsley, to garnish

MUSTARD BASTE
1 tablespoon coarse-grain mustard (see Buying guide)
½ teaspoon ground ginger
2 teaspoons light soy sauce
1 clove garlic, crushed (optional)
2 teaspoons olive or vegetable oil

1 Place lamb chops in a roasting tin and season with salt and pepper.
2 Make the mustard baste: in a small bowl, beat together mustard, ginger, soy sauce and garlic, if using. Add the oil, a few drops at a time, until it is incorporated.
3 Spread baste over top of chops. Set aside the coated chops in a cool place for 2 hours.
4 Heat the oven to 190C/375F/Gas 5.
5 Put roasting tin into the oven and cook the chops for 25 minutes, turning once.
6 Transfer the chops to a warmed serving plate, garnish with the fresh parsley and serve at once.

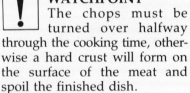

Scallop and bacon kebabs

SERVES 4

500 g/1 lb frozen scallops, defrosted and halved (see Buying guide)
150 ml/¼ pint fish stock (see Variations)
salt and freshly ground black pepper
3 tablespoons finely chopped fresh parsley
1 clove garlic, finely chopped (optional)
10 slices streaky bacon, rinds removed, stretched with the back of a knife and halved
40 g/1½ oz butter, melted
4 lemon wedges, to garnish

1 Put the scallops into a saucepan and pour over the fish stock. Season with salt and pepper.
2 Bring to the boil over moderate heat, then lower the heat, cover the pan and simmer for 5 minutes. Drain the scallops well and pat them dry with absorbent paper.
3 Spread out the parsley and garlic, if using, on a flat plate. Roll the scallops in the parsley until evenly covered. Set aside.
4 Heat the grill to high.
5 Roll up pieces of bacon neatly. Thread the pieces of scallop and the streaky bacon rolls alternately on to 4 long metal kebab skewers.
6 Place the kebabs on the grill rack and brush with melted butter. Grill for 10-12 minutes, turning the kebabs frequently.
7 Arrange the kebabs on a warmed serving plate. Garnish with lemon wedges and serve at once, while still hot (see Serving ideas).

Cook's Notes

 TIME
Preparation takes about 20 minutes and cooking the kebabs 10-12 minutes.

 BUYING GUIDE
Use large frozen scallops which can be cut in half to give enough pieces. Some scallops may have the pink roe, coral as it is called, still attached. This can be left on.

 VARIATIONS
Fish stock cubes are available from some delicatessens. If they are difficult to obtain, use homemade chicken stock or ¼ chicken stock cube.

The kebabs can be cooked on a barbecue, if wished. Baste them frequently, adding extra butter, if necessary.

 SERVING IDEAS
Serve the scallop and bacon kebabs with a tasty mixed salad or, alternatively, on a bed of boiled rice.

●250 calories/1050 kj per portion

Italian-style kidneys

SERVES 4

8 lamb kidneys, skinned
25 g/1 oz margarine or butter
1 tablespoon vegetable oil
1 large onion, finely chopped
1 clove garlic, crushed (optional)
1 large red pepper, deseeded and
    coarsely chopped
100 g/4 oz button mushrooms,
    sliced
125 ml/4 fl oz red wine or beef stock
4 tomatoes, skinned, chopped and
    deseeded
1 tablespoon tomato purée
1/2 teaspoon dried oregano
salt and freshly ground black pepper
12 stuffed olives, halved

1 Cut the kidneys in half horizontally and remove the cores with a small, sharp knife or kitchen scissors. Slice into bite-sized pieces.
2 Heat the margarine and oil in a large frying-pan with a lid and fry the kidneys for about 3 minutes until firm, turning once. ⚠ Remove the kidneys from the pan with a slotted spoon and reserve.
3 Add the onion and garlic, if using, to the pan and fry gently, stirring occasionally, for about 5 minutes until soft and lightly coloured. Add the red pepper and mushrooms and fry for 3 minutes, stirring occasionally, then stir in the wine or stock, tomatoes, tomato purée and oregano. Mix well and season to taste with salt and pepper. Lay olives on top, add kidneys.
4 Cover the pan and cook gently for about 10 minutes until the kidneys are just tender, turning them over in the sauce once or twice during cooking. ⚠ Taste and adjust seasoning, then serve at once.

Cook's Notes

TIME
Preparation takes 10-15 minutes, cooking 20 minutes.

SERVING IDEAS
Serve on a bed of boiled rice. Broccoli garnished with fried breadcrumbs, or aubergines or courgettes fried in butter and garnished with chopped parsley would make good vegetable accompaniments.

VARIATIONS
If you do not like the taste of garlic, use 1/2 teaspoon Worcestershire sauce, or 1 teaspoon French mustard instead.

WATCHPOINT
It is important to cook the kidneys over low heat. Do not overcook or they will harden and become dry.

●220 calories/925 kj per portion

SALADS

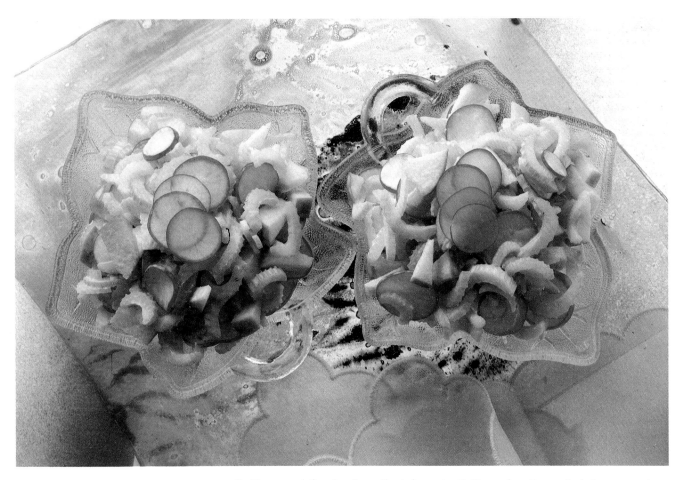

Celery and radish salad

SERVES 4

1 crisp dessert apple
1 small head celery, finely chopped
250 g/9 oz radishes, thinly sliced
   (see Buying guide)
salt and freshly ground black pepper

DRESSING
50 g/2 oz curd cheese
4 tablespoons soured cream
2 tablespoons cider vinegar
1 teaspoon light soft brown sugar
1 clove garlic, crushed (optional)

1 Make the dressing: put the curd cheese into a large bowl and beat until softened. Gradually beat in the soured cream and vinegar, then the sugar and garlic, if using.

2 Core and finely chop (but do not peel) the apple. Add to the dressing with the celery and half the radishes and mix well, adding salt and pepper to taste.

3 Transfer the salad to a serving bowl and arrange the remaining radishes on top in an attractive pattern. Serve as soon as possible, at room temperature.

Cook's Notes

TIME
Preparation takes 25 minutes.

VARIATIONS
Cream cheese may be used instead of curd cheese, and natural yoghurt instead of soured cream.

BUYING GUIDE
The average bunch of radishes available from greengrocers weighs about 100 g/4 oz, so you will need 2 bunches for this recipe.

SERVING IDEAS
This salad goes perfectly with a quiche for lunch, or with cold chicken or turkey. It also makes an attractive starter salad as shown in the photograph, served with Melba toast and butter.

DID YOU KNOW
Celery is rich in mineral salts, vitamins and iron, and is one of the best vegetables for slimmers.

●70 calories/300 kj per portion

Oriental seafood salad

SERVES 4

250 g/9 oz beansprouts
4 spring onions, chopped
1 celery stalk, finely sliced
1 red pepper, deseeded and cut into 5 mm/¼ inch strips (optional)
100 g/4 oz peeled prawns, defrosted if frozen (see Economy)
175 g/6 oz can crabmeat, drained and flaked
6 Chinese leaves or lettuce leaves
spring onion tassels, to garnish

DRESSING

150 g/5 oz natural yoghurt
6 tablespoons thick bottled mayonnaise
finely grated zest of 1 lemon
1 tablespoon lemon juice
1 teaspoon ground ginger
salt and freshly ground black pepper

Cook's Notes

 TIME
Preparation takes only 15 minutes plus 15-30 minutes chilling time.

 SERVING IDEAS
Serve this refreshing salad with fried prawn crackers available from many large supermarkets. Alternatively, serve as a starter to a Chinese-style meal – it will make 6 servings. Follow salad with a main course of stir-fried vegetables with beef or pork strips and a bowl of rice. Shred some of the leftover Chinese leaves and add to the vegetables.

ECONOMY
Omit the prawns and use 200 g/7 oz can drained sweetcorn instead. Or you can substitute a 200 g/7 oz can tuna, drained and flaked, for the canned crabmeat.

●250 calories/1050 kj per portion

1 Combine the beansprouts, spring onions and celery in a bowl with the red pepper, if using.
2 Make the dressing: put the yoghurt in a bowl with the mayonnaise, lemon zest and juice and ginger. Mix together and season with salt and pepper to taste.
3 Add the dressing to the bean- sprouts mixture and toss to coat well, then fold the prawns and crabmeat into the salad. Cover with cling film and refrigerate the salad for about 15-30 minutes.
4 Arrange the Chinese leaves on a serving plate and spoon the salad on top. Garnish with spring onion tassels and serve at once.

Cauliflower salad with sultanas

SERVES 6

1 cauliflower, broken into florets
500 g/1 lb small button onions (see Preparation)
salt
225 ml/8 fl oz white wine
125 ml/4 fl oz water
5 tablespoons olive oil
2 tablespoons wine vinegar
3 tomatoes, skinned, deseeded and chopped
3 tablespoons sultanas
1 teaspoon Demerara sugar
½ teaspoon dried thyme
½ teaspoon ground coriander
freshly ground black pepper

1 Bring 2 pans of salted water to the boil and blanch the cauliflower florets and onions separately for 5 minutes. Drain both together in a colander, then rinse under cold running water to refresh. Drain the vegetables again.

2 Put the remaining ingredients in a large pan with salt to taste and a generous sprinkling of black pepper. Stir well to mix, bring to the boil and boil for 5 minutes.

3 Lower the heat, add the cauliflower and onions and simmer for a further 8 minutes, turning the vegetables occasionally.

4 Using a slotted spoon, transfer the vegetables to a serving dish. Bring the sauce left in the pan to the boil and boil for 5 minutes to reduce slightly. Pour the sauce over the vegetables and leave until cold. Serve at room temperature.

Cook's Notes

 TIME
Preparation 10 minutes, cooking about 20 minutes, but allow time for cooling the salad before serving.

 WATCHPOINT
Be careful not to over-cook the cauliflower florets. Test them with the point of a knife during cooking to check that they are still crisp.

PREPARATION
Cut off the ends of the onions and remove the skins: keep the onions whole.

SERVING IDEAS
This is an ideal dish for a starter as it can be prepared in advance. Serve with warm French bread.

● 175 calories/725 kj per portion

Stuffed tomato salad

SERVES 4

 4 large tomatoes
250 g/9 oz fennel bulb
 175 g/6 oz cucumber
250 g/9 oz radishes
1 tablespoon chopped fresh parsley

DRESSING
6 tablespoons olive oil
1 tablespoon lemon juice
½ teaspoon clear honey
½ teaspoon salt
**generous sprinkling of freshly
    ground black pepper**

1 Trim the fennel and finely chop 1 tablespoon of the leaves. Reserve the remaining whole fennel leaves for the garnish.
2 Cut the fennel bulb into eighths, then slice thinly. Peel cucumber, cut it into quarters lengthways,

then slice thinly. Cut the radishes into very thin slices.
3 Cut off tops of the tomatoes, then scoop out the flesh and seeds with a teaspoon, taking care not to break the skins (see Economy).
4 Put all the dressing ingredients into a screw-top jar and shake well to mix thoroughly.
5 Put sliced fennel bulb, cucumber

and the radishes into a bowl with the parsley and the finely chopped fennel leaves. Pour the dressing over the salad and toss the contents thoroughly to mix well.
6 Arrange the tomatoes in individual dishes, and spoon the salad into them. Garnish with the reserved fennel leaves and serve at once (see Serving ideas).

Cook's Notes

 TIME
The stuffed tomatoes take 20 minutes to prepare and 5 minutes to assemble and garnish.

SERVING IDEAS
These tomatoes make a delicious snack served on their own with French bread. They also make an attractive addition to buffets and are excellent with sliced cold roast meat.

ECONOMY
The pulp which is scooped out from these large tomatoes is excellent for adding to casseroles or for giving extra flavour and colour to soups and sauces.

 WATCHPOINT
Serve the tomatoes as soon as possible after filling or they may soften.

●225 calories/950 kj per portion

Egg and lettuce salad

SERVES 6

1 crisp lettuce, shredded (see Buying guide)
1 bunch spring onions, chopped
4 hard-boiled egg whites, finely chopped, to garnish

DRESSING

4 warm hard-boiled egg yolks (see Cook's tip)
150 ml/¼ pint soured cream
1 teaspoon sugar
juice of 2 lemons
salt and freshly ground black pepper

1 Make the dressing: put the warm egg yolks in a bowl with a little of the soured cream and mix to a paste with a fork. Add the sugar, lemon juice and the remaining soured cream. Whisk with the fork until the dressing is smooth and the ingredients are thoroughly combined. Season to taste with salt and pepper.

2 Place the shredded lettuce in a large salad bowl. Sprinkle the spring onions over the lettuce, then pour the dressing over the top of the salad.

3 Toss well to coat the lettuce thoroughly with the dressing, then garnish the salad with the finely chopped egg whites. Serve at once while lettuce is crisp.

Cook's Notes

 TIME
This salad takes 20 minutes to make.

 COOK'S TIP
It is best to make the dressing when the yolks are still warm; they are softer and will mash more easily.

 BUYING GUIDE
The best type of lettuce to buy for this dish is a crisp iceberg, but if unavailable use a Webb or cos lettuce.

●120 calories/500 kj per portion

Beetroot and pear salad

SERVES 4

 175 g/6 oz cooked beetroot, peeled and cut into 1 cm/½ inch dice (see Cook's tips)
 2 medium pears
½ head fennel, trimmed and chopped (optional)
1 bunch watercress, stalks discarded

DRESSING
grated zest and juice of ½ lemon
1 tablespoon natural yoghurt
1 tablespoon vegetable oil
1 teaspoon clear honey
½ teaspoon wine vinegar
salt and freshly ground black pepper

1 First make the dressing: in a large bowl mix the lemon zest and juice with the yoghurt, oil, honey and vinegar. Season with salt and pepper and whisk until combined.

2 Peel, halve and core the pears, then dice and add to the dressing with the beetroot and fennel, if using. Turn the mixture over gently to coat thoroughly.

3 Cover the salad with cling film and refrigerate until needed. When ready to serve, tear the watercress leaves into small pieces and gently fold them into the salad. Pile the salad into a serving dish and serve at once.

Cook's Notes

 TIME
Preparation 30 minutes. Allow 2 hours for chilling before serving.

SERVING IDEAS
This salad goes very well with any cold meat, or as part of a mixed hors d'oeuvre selection.

VARIATIONS
If pears are not available, try substituting apples. Soured cream may be used instead of yoghurt. If you do not like the aniseed flavour of fennel, use celery, which has the same crunchy texture.

WATCHPOINT
Pears discolour quickly once they are peeled, so make the dressing first and dice the pears directly into it. The lemon juice will prevent them turning brown.

COOK'S TIPS
You can buy ready-cooked beetroot from most greengrocers and supermarkets (peel it if the skin is still on). If you choose to cook your own, run the beetroot under cold water when it is cooked, to make it easier to peel.

● 100 calories/400 kj per portion

Brussels sprouts and date salad

SERVES 6

500 g/1 lb Brussels sprouts
250 g/9 oz carrots, grated
100 g/4 oz stoned dates, chopped

DRESSING
150 g/5 oz natural yoghurt, chilled
2 tablespoons mayonnaise
2 tablespoons fresh orange juice
salt and freshly ground black pepper
2 tablespoons snipped chives

TO SERVE
2 heads chicory or 1 lettuce heart,
trimmed and separated into
leaves
25 g/1 oz walnut halves (optional)

1 Trim the sprouts, discarding any tough or discoloured outer leaves. Wash and drain them thoroughly, tossing them in a clean tea-towel or on absorbent paper.
2 Shred the sprouts with a sharp knife, then place in a large mixing bowl with the grated carrots and dates. Mix well to combine.
3 To make the dressing: beat together the yoghurt, mayonnaise and orange juice. Add salt and pepper to taste, then stir in the chives.
4 Pour the dressing over the vegetables and mix well. Taste and adjust seasoning. Cover and refrigerate for about 1 hour, or longer.
5 To serve: line a deep serving bowl with the chicory or lettuce leaves, then spoon the chilled salad into the centre, piling it up in a mound. Garnish with the walnuts, if using.

Cook's Notes

 TIME
45 minutes preparation, plus at least 1 hour chilling.

 SERVING IDEAS
This unusual salad has a slightly 'tangy' flavour, and makes a refreshing first course. It is also a good accompaniment to mixed cold meats, continental sausages, or cold meat pies.

VARIATIONS
Use 2 tablespoons each seedless raisins and sultanas instead of the dates.

●145 calories/600 kj per portion

Meat ball salad

SERVES 4

500 g/1 lb lean minced beef
4 large button mushrooms, cut into
    quarters
2 tablespoons grated onion
2 tablespoons tomato relish or
    chutney
¼ teaspoon dried marjoram or
    mixed herbs
50 g/2 oz fresh white breadcrumbs
1 egg, beaten
2 tomatoes, cut into eighths (see
    Variation)
1 small round lettuce, shredded
1 green pepper, deseeded and
    sliced into rings
½ cucumber, thinly sliced
vegetable oil, for brushing

MARINADE
3 tablespoons vegetable oil
1 tablespoon lemon juice
1 clove garlic, crushed (optional)
salt and freshly ground black pepper

1 Make the marinade: combine the oil, lemon juice and garlic, if using, in a bowl. Season to taste with salt and pepper. Add the mushrooms, toss thoroughly and leave them to marinate for at least 1 hour.
2 Meanwhile, heat the grill to high.
3 Mix together the minced beef, grated onion, tomato relish, herbs and breadcrumbs. Season to taste with salt and pepper and add enough beaten egg to bind the mixture (about 1 tablespoon).
4 Divide the mixture into 16 portions and form each into a ball.

Brush with oil and place on the rack in the grill pan.
5 Grill the meat balls for 15-20 minutes, turning as necessary, until brown and cooked through. Drain on absorbent paper, then set aside to cool for 30 minutes.
6 Arrange the lettuce, green pepper and cucumber on a serving plate.
7 Using a slotted spoon, transfer the mushrooms from the marinade to a plate. Thread the meat balls, tomatoes and mushrooms on to cocktail sticks and arrange next to the salad. Serve at once.

Cook's Notes

TIME
Preparation and cooking the meat balls take 35 minutes, plus marinating. Allow 30 minutes cooling time and 10 minutes to finish the dish.

VARIATION
Use 16 cherry tomatoes, if available, instead of the ordinary salad tomatoes.

SERVING IDEAS
This salad makes a delicious summer lunch or supper dish.
   It can also be served hot as kebabs: grill the mushrooms, tomatoes and meat balls on metal skewers and serve them on a bed of plain boiled rice.

●300 calories/1250 kj per portion

Creamy potato salad

SERVES 4

750 g/1½ lb potatoes, scrubbed (see Buying guide)
salt

DRESSING
150 ml/¼ pint soured cream
2 tablespoons capers, rinsed and drained
4 spring onions, thinly sliced
½ teaspoon lemon juice
freshly ground black pepper

TO GARNISH
4-8 spring onion tassels (see Preparation)
1 tablespoon chopped fresh mint

1 Bring the potatoes to the boil in salted water and simmer for 15-20 minutes, or until they are just tender.

2 Meanwhile, prepare the spring onion tassels and leave them to curl in a bowl of iced water for at least 30 minutes.

3 Make the dressing: mix all the ingredients together in a bowl with salt and pepper to taste.

4 Drain the potatoes, leave until cool enough to handle, then remove the skins and dice the flesh.

5 Toss the potatoes in the dressing while they are still warm, then leave them to cool completely.

6 Serve the potato salad when it has just cooled, garnished with spring onion tassels and chopped mint.

Cook's Notes

 TIME
15 minutes preparation, about 20 minutes cooking, plus cooling time.

 PREPARATION
To prepare a spring onion tassel: trim off the roots, peel off the thin outer skin and cut off most of the green top. Using a very sharp knife, cut several slits close together from the top of the onion down to within about 2.5 cm/1 inch of the bottom of the bulb. Repeat with the remaining onions.

 VARIATIONS
This salad can also be served hot. Return the diced cooked potato to the pan with the soured cream, capers and lemon juice and season to taste with salt and pepper. Heat gently until the dressing is on the point of boiling. Stir in the spring onions just before serving, so that they retain their crispness.

 BUYING GUIDE
Choose a potato that will hold its shape—Desirée is the ideal variety for this recipe.

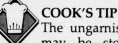 **COOK'S TIP**
The ungarnished salad may be stored in a covered container in the refrigerator. Allow to come to room temperature before serving.

●240 calories/1000 kj per portion

Autumn salad

SERVES 4

3 dessert apples (see Buying guide)
1 onion, thinly sliced and separated into rings
425 g/15 oz can butter beans, drained
50 g/2 oz walnut pieces
sprigs of mint, to garnish

DRESSING
150 g/5 oz natural yoghurt
1 tablespoon chopped mint
2 teaspoons lemon juice
salt and freshly ground black pepper

1 Make the dressing: mix yoghurt, mint and lemon juice in a large bowl and season to taste with salt and pepper.
2 Quarter, core and thinly slice the apples and then toss them in the yoghurt dressing until well coated.
3 Add the onion, butter beans and walnuts to the bowl and toss together. Turn the salad into a serving bowl, garnish with mint and serve at once.

Cook's Notes

 TIME
This refreshing salad takes only 20 minutes to prepare and dress.

BUYING GUIDE
To give the salad some colour, choose a red-skinned apple such as Red Delicious or Worcester.

 VARIATIONS
To make a more substantial lunch dish, add 50 g/2 oz diced ham or cheese to the salad.
For a different dressing, use mayonnaise instead of yoghurt and double the lemon juice.

●190 calories/800 kj per portion

Watercress and grapefruit salad

SERVES 4

2 bunches watercress, stalks removed (see Cook's tip)
2 pink grapefruits, divided into segments (see Buying guide and Preparation)
50 g/2 oz split almonds

DRESSING
1 teaspoon finely chopped onion
½ teaspoon sugar
juice of 1 fresh lime
2 tablespoons olive oil
salt and freshly ground black pepper

1 Heat the grill to moderate and spread the almonds in the grill pan. Toast them for 8-10 minutes, turning from time to time, until they are golden brown.
2 To make the dressing: put the onion, sugar, lime juice and olive oil in a salad bowl. Whisk with a fork until the dressing is thick and all the ingredients are thoroughly combined. Season with salt and pepper.
3 Stir the grapefruit segments and any juice in the bowl into the dressing, add the watercress leaves and toss together.
4 Sprinkle the toasted almonds over the salad and serve at once.

Cook's Notes

TIME
This salad takes 25 minutes to make, including the time for toasting the almonds.

BUYING GUIDE
Pink grapefruits are the sweetest type of grapefruit you can buy; if not available, use ordinary yellow grapefruit and increase the quantity of sugar to 1 teaspoon.

COOK'S TIP
Watercress will keep well for up to 1 week in the salad drawer of the refrigerator—put the trimmed and washed watercress in a plastic bag, excluding as much air as possible.

SERVING IDEAS
Serve as a starter with Melba toast, or as an accompaniment to grilled steaks and chops.

PREPARATION
Peel the grapefruit, holding it over a bowl to catch the juice. Trim away the pith with a small, sharp knife then divide into segments. Remove the pips.

●155 calories/650 kj per portion

Harvest ham salad

SERVES 4

250 g/9 oz cooked ham, diced
600 ml/1 pint water
salt
150 g/5 oz fresh peas (shelled
    weight)
250 g/9 oz courgettes, sliced
    diagonally into 1 cm/½ inch
    lengths
2 tablespoons thick bottled
    mayonnaise
4 tablespoons natural yoghurt
½ teaspoon mustard powder
freshly ground black pepper
250 g/9 oz white cabbage, finely
    shredded
snipped chives, to garnish

1 Bring the water to the boil in a saucepan, add salt to taste, then the peas. Bring back to the boil, then lower the heat, cover and simmer for 3 minutes.
2 Add the sliced courgettes to the pan, cover again and simmer for a further 4-5 minutes until the vegetables are just tender. Drain, rinse under cold running water, then spread out on absorbent paper to cool and drain thoroughly.
3 In a large bowl, mix the mayonnaise, yoghurt and mustard with salt and pepper to taste. Fold in the cabbage, ham, peas and courgettes.
4 Turn the mixture into a serving dish and garnish with snipped chives. Serve at once or place ungarnished in a covered container and refrigerate overnight, then garnish just before serving.

Cook's Notes

 TIME
Total preparation time is about 20 minutes.

 VARIATIONS
Frozen peas can be used, but need less cooking time. Put them into the boiling water with the courgettes.
  Other cooked meats can be used in place of ham. Try chicken, salami or smoked continental sausage.

 SERVING IDEAS
Serve with French or fresh pitta bread.

● 210 calories/875 kj per portion

44

Carrot and coconut salad

SERVES 4-6

500 g/1 lb carrots
juice of 1 orange
juice of 1 lemon
50 g/2 oz desiccated coconut

1 Grate the carrots using either a hand grater or food processor (see Cook's tip). Put the grated carrots in a large bowl.
2 Mix the orange and lemon juice together, then pour over the carrots. Toss the salad well.
3 Transfer the carrots and juice to a salad bowl or divide the salad between individual serving dishes and sprinkle over the coconut.

4 Chill the carrot and coconut salad in the refrigerator for at least 1 hour or until ready to serve.

Cook's Notes

TIME
The salad takes 10 minutes to prepare, plus chilling time.

SERVING IDEAS
Serve this refreshingly tangy salad with cold roast chicken or pork. It is particularly good for slimmers, since no sweetening is necessary. Coconut shells make unusual serving dishes.

COOK'S TIP
To make grating easier, crisp the carrots by soaking them whole in iced water for 1 hour before.

VARIATION
Toss the salad in an oil and vinegar dressing instead of the lemon and orange juice mixture.

●120 calories/500 kj per portion

Mushroom and celery salad

SERVES 4
250 g/9 oz button mushrooms,
   sliced
3 celery stalks, sliced

DRESSING
150 g/5 oz natural yoghurt
2 tablespoons olive oil
2 tablespoons lemon juice
1 teaspoon finely chopped fresh
   tarragon (see Buying guide)
salt and freshly ground black pepper

TO GARNISH
25 g/1 oz flaked almonds, toasted
lemon wedges (optional)
few sprigs of fresh tarragon
   (optional)

1 Make the dressing: put the yoghurt in a bowl with the olive oil and lemon juice. Beat together with a fork, then stir in the tarragon and salt and pepper to taste.
2 Add the mushrooms and celery to the dressing and stir well to ensure the vegetables are thoroughly and evenly coated.
3 Turn the salad into a serving bowl and sprinkle with the toasted almonds. Garnish with the lemon wedges and tarragon sprigs, if using, and serve at once.

Cook's Notes

TIME
This light salad takes 20-25 minutes to make.

SERVING IDEAS
Try serving this salad as a refreshing starter or as an accompaniment to cold meat.

VARIATION
Replace the tarragon with 1-2 crushed garlic cloves—beat into the yoghurt with the olive oil and lemon juice, then taste and adjust the seasoning.

BUYING GUIDE
It is better to use fresh rather than dried herbs, both for the flavour and the appearance. If fresh tarragon is unobtainable, substitute with either fresh parsley or chives.

●125 calories/525 kj per portion

Buckling and beetroot salad

SERVES 4

2 buckling (see Buying guide)
10 cm/4 inch piece of cucumber
250 g/9 oz cooked beetroot, cut into 5 mm/¼ inch rounds and then into neat strips
2 teaspoons vegetable oil
1 teaspoon cider or white wine vinegar
12 lettuce leaves, to serve
4 gherkins, cut into fan shapes and 4 sprigs of watercress, to garnish

1 Remove the skin from the buckling and carefully pick the flesh from the bones. Flake the flesh into a large bowl. If the fish has roes, cut these into neat pieces and add them to the flesh.

2 Cut the piece of cucumber across into 4 equal slices, then cut each slice into strips.

3 Add the cucumber and the remaining ingredients, except the lettuce and gherkins and watercress, to the buckling and toss together lightly with a fork.

4 Arrange lettuce leaves on each of 4 individual serving plates. Pile the buckling mixture into the centre. Garnish salad with a gherkin fan and watercress and serve at once.

Cook's Notes

TIME
This tasty and colourful salad takes only about 10 minutes to prepare.

SERVING IDEAS
Serve this salad as an unusual light lunch.

BUYING GUIDE
Buckling are smoked herrings and can be bought from fishmongers, supermarkets and delicatessens.

● 195 calories/800 kj per portion

Chinese leaf salad

SERVES 4

250 g/9 oz Chinese leaves, shredded (see Preparation)
100 g/4 oz mushrooms, sliced
4 large spring onions, chopped

DRESSING
4 tablespoons corn oil
2 tablespoons wine vinegar
1 tablespoon soy sauce

1 First make the dressing: put the oil, vinegar and soy sauce in a large bowl and beat together with a fork until well mixed.
2 Add the mushrooms and onions; toss so that they are thoroughly coated in dressing. Cover and leave to marinate for at least 15 minutes.

Cook's Notes

 TIME
Easy to make, this tangy salad only requires 10 minutes preparation, plus marinating time.

 SERVING IDEAS
This salad is excellent for adding interest to cold meats—it is particularly good with pork or ham.

VARIATION
To make the salad more substantial, add 100 g/4 oz chopped cooked ham, garlic sausage or salami with the Chinese leaves.

PREPARATION
To shred the Chinese leaves:

Cut the leaves in half lengthways (quarter them if large), then slice across to shred them.

●135 calories/575 kj per portion

3 Turn the mushroom mixture into a large salad bowl and surround with the shredded Chinese leaves. Toss together thoroughly.

DESSERTS

Lemon layer sponge

SERVES 4

3 large eggs, separated
3 tablespoons plain flour
3 tablespoons caster sugar
175 ml/6 fl oz milk
25 g/1 oz butter, melted
grated zest and juice of 1 lemon
icing sugar, to dredge
pouring cream, to serve

1 Heat the oven to 170C/325F/Gas 3.
2 Place the egg yolks, flour, caster sugar, milk, butter and lemon zest in a large bowl and whisk until smoothly blended.
3 In a clean dry bowl, and using clean beaters, whisk the egg whites until stiff. Gently but thoroughly fold them into the lemon mixture, using a large metal spoon.
4 Spoon the mixture into a buttered 1 L/2 pint baking dish standing in a roasting tin. Pour enough hot water into the tin to come about 2.5 cm/1 inch up the side of the dish (see Preparation).
5 Bake the pudding in the oven for about 1 hour until risen, golden, and just firm to the touch. Remove the dish from the tin. Sift icing sugar thickly over the top of the pudding. Serve while still warm, with cream.

Cook's Notes

TIME
About 15 minutes to prepare and 1 hour to bake.

PREPARATION
Standing the dish in a tin of hot water for baking helps keep the pudding deliciously soft and moist.
During baking, the mixture separates into layers: a light sponge on top and a rich custard sauce underneath.

● 210 calories/875 kj per portion

Mango yoghurt foam

SERVES 4
 1 orange
 2 large, ripe mangoes, sliced (see Preparation)
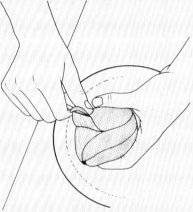 1 teaspoon powdered gelatine
3 tablespoons cold water
300 ml/½ pint thick natural yoghurt
2-3 tablespoons caster sugar
1 egg white

1 Using a potato peeler, pare several strips of zest from the orange. ☐ With a small, sharp knife, shred the zest into matchstick-sized strips.
2 Bring a small pan of water to the boil and blanch the strips for 2-3 minutes; drain and refresh under cold running water. Drain again, then pat dry on absorbent paper and set aside.
3 Squeeze the juice from the orange, then purée the prepared mangoes and orange juice in a blender, or work the mangoes through a nylon sieve and stir in the orange juice.
4 Sprinkle the gelatine over the water in a small, heavy-based pan. Leave to soak for 5 minutes, then set over very low heat for 1-2 minutes, until the gelatine is dissolved.
5 Stirring constantly with a wooden spoon, pour the dissolved gelatine in a thin stream on to the mango purée (see Cook's tip). Gradually beat in the yoghurt, then sweeten to taste with caster sugar.
6 In a spotlessly clean, dry bowl, whisk the egg white until standing in stiff peaks. Using a large metal spoon, fold the egg white into the mango mixture. Taste and fold in more caster sugar, if necessary.
7 Spoon the foam into 4 dessert dishes or stemmed glasses and decorate with the strips of orange zest. Serve within 2 hours.

Cook's Notes

 TIME
Preparation takes about 50 minutes.

WATCHPOINT
Take care to remove only the coloured zest and not the bitter white pith just beneath it.

PREPARATION
Peel mangoes over a plate (to catch the juices) as shown below, then slice the flesh from the large central stone in large pieces. Scrape any remaining flesh from the skin and add to the slices, together with any juices.

Score the skin lengthways with a small, sharp knife, dividing it into several sections. Hold a corner of one section between the flat side of the blade and your thumb, then pull the skin away from the flesh. Remove the remaining sections of skin in the same way.

 COOK'S TIP
Use a flexible rubber spatula to scrape the last of the dissolved gelatine out of the pan.

VARIATIONS
If fresh mangoes are unavailable, use two 250 g/9 oz cans well-drained mango slices. Other soft or drained canned fruits can be used instead of mangoes: you will need 300 ml/½ pint thick purée.

●150 calories/625 kj per portion

Pineapple and grape salads

SERVES 6

25-50 g/1-2 oz sugar
150 ml/¼ pint water
150 ml/¼ pint dry white wine
2 small pineapples
350 g/12 oz black grapes, halved,
  pips removed

1 Put the sugar and water into a saucepan and heat gently until the sugar has dissolved. Stir in the wine, pour into a bowl and cool.

2 Leave the leafy tops on the pineapples and cut them into 3 wedges. Using a sharp stainless steel knife, carefully cut away the flesh, about 1 cm/½ inch from the outer skin. ! Dice the flesh and stir into the syrup with the grape halves.

3 To serve: place pineapple shells on serving dishes and fill with fruit. Spoon over the syrup, cover and refrigerate for at least 1 hour.

Cook's Notes

TIME
Preparation 20 minutes. Chilling time 1 hour.

SERVING IDEAS
Serve with natural yoghurt.

WATCHPOINT
Be careful not to cut right through the pineapple skin, or the syrup will gradually leak out.

●155 calories/650 kj per portion

Spiced pears

SERVES 6

425 ml/¾ pint dry cider
75 g/3 oz apricot jam, sieved
40 g/1½ oz soft brown sugar
¼ teaspoon ground cinnamon
2 whole cloves
6 firm pears
thin strips of orange zest
juice of ½ lemon
3 tablespoons flaked almonds,
  toasted (optional)

1 Bring the cider, jam, sugar and spices slowly to the boil in a deep saucepan.
2 Peel the pears, leaving them whole and with the stalks on. Immediately stand them upright in the saucepan, add the orange zest and lemon juice, cover tightly and simmer gently for 20-30 minutes or until just tender but not too soft (see Cook's tip).
3 Cut a thin slice from the base of each pear. Stand the pears upright in a serving dish. Boil the liquid in the uncovered saucepan for about 10 minutes to reduce by half. Strain and pour over the pears. Leave overnight to soak in the refrigerator or in a cool place. About 1 hour before serving, baste the pears well with the syrup.
4 Sprinkle the almonds over the pears just before serving.

Cook's Notes

TIME
Preparation and cooking take 40 minutes. Allow for soaking overnight.

COOK'S TIP
This is a good way of using hard pears. Cooking time will depend on the hardness of the fruit.

SERVING IDEAS
Serve with whipped cream and crisp biscuits. Almond biscuits go particularly well with pears.

PRESSURE COOKING
Cook the pears at high pressure for 1 minute.

VARIATIONS
Use red or white wine instead of cider and substitute 50 g/2 oz sugar for the jam. To use canned pear halves instead of fresh pears, boil the other ingredients together until the mixture is reduced by half, pour over the well-drained fruit and soak.

●125 calories/525 kj per portion

Rhubarb banana whip

SERVES 4

540 g/1 lb 3 oz can rhubarb in syrup,
   drained (see Cook's tips)
2 small bananas, chopped
150 g/5 oz natural yoghurt
few drops of red edible food
   colouring
1 egg white

1 Purée the rhubarb with the bananas and yoghurt in a blender (see Cook's tips). Pour into a large bowl and stir in a few drops of food colouring to tint the mixture pink.
2 Whisk the egg white until stiff, then fold into the rhubarb mixture using a large metal spoon.
3 Divide the mixture between 4 dishes, cover and chill for at least 2 hours; top with banana if wished.

Cook's Notes

TIME
Preparation takes about 15 minutes, but remember to allow 2 hours for chilling.

COOK'S TIPS
When in season, use 500 g/1 lb fresh rhubarb, stewed, drained and sweetened, instead of canned fruit.

If you do not have a blender or processor, use a fork to mash the rhubarb and bananas to a pulp, then beat in the yoghurt.

Canned rhubarb varies in sweetness; taste the mixture before folding in the egg white, and, if necessary, stir in a little caster sugar.

This dessert will keep in the refrigerator for up to 4 hours.

SERVING IDEAS
Banana slices, dipped in lemon juice to prevent discoloration, can be used to decorate the dessert. Serve with shortbread biscuits for texture contrast.

●80 calories/325 kj per portion

Cranberry sherbet in apple cases

SERVES 6

2 × 180 g/6½ oz jars cranberry
   sauce
finely grated zest of 1 small orange
2 egg whites
6 green dessert apples
2 tablespoons lemon juice
apple leaves, to decorate (optional)

1 Press the cranberry sauce through a sieve into a bowl. Add the orange zest, stir well to mix, then refrigerate for 30 minutes.
2 In a clean dry bowl, whisk the egg whites until standing in soft peaks, then fold into the cranberry and orange mixture.
3 Pour into a shallow freezerproof container and freeze (see Cook's tip) for about 1 hour or until the mixture is firm around the edges.
4 Remove from the freezer, turn out into a bowl and beat well until smooth. Return the mixture to the

---

Cook's Notes

TIME
About 35 minutes to prepare sherbet and 5 hours freezing; then about 30 minutes to prepare apples and 30 minutes final freezing.

COOK'S TIP
If using the freezing compartment of the refrigerator, turn to coldest setting 1 hour before making the sherbet. Return it to the original setting afterwards.

● 170 calories/700 kj per portion

PREPARATION
Hollow out an apple as follows:

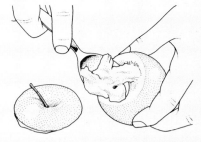

Cut top off apple then, using a sharp-edged teaspoon cut out core, leaving a 1 cm/½ inch thick shell.

---

freezerproof container and continue to freeze for at least 4 hours until it is quite solid.
5 Remove sherbet from the freezer and stand at room temperature for about 30 minutes until it is soft enough to scoop.
6 Meanwhile, hollow out the centre of each apple to within 1 cm/½ inch of the base (see Preparation).

Immediately brush the insides of apples with lemon juice and refrigerate until required.
7 Fill the apple cavities with scoops of the sherbet, stand on a baking sheet and return to the freezer for about 30 minutes until the apples begin to look frosty. Decorate with apple tops or leaves, if liked, and stand on individual plates. Serve.

Sliced oranges in syrup

SERVES 6

9 juicy oranges, preferably seedless
75-100 g/3-4 oz sugar
grated zest and juice of 1 lemon

1 Peel the oranges using a fine serrated knife to remove the rind, pith and thin white membrane, leaving the flesh exposed (see Preparation).
2 Cut the oranges horizontally into thin slices with a sharp knife, removing any pips.
3 Arrange the orange slices in layers in a large glass serving dish, sprinkling each layer with some of the sugar, a little of the grated lemon zest and lemon juice.
4 Cover and refrigerate for at least 4 hours. Serve well chilled.

Cook's Notes

TIME
Preparation takes about 30 minutes. Prepare at least 4 hours in advance to allow time for the flavours to blend.

PREPARATION
Peeling the oranges: peel over a bowl to catch the juices. Use a fine serrated knife and make a sawing movement to remove the rind, together with pith and white membrane with a single cut.
Grate the lemon zest (the thin outer skin with aromatic oils) very finely, avoiding any of the bitter white pith.

SPECIAL OCCASION
Add 3-4 tablespoons of an orange liqueur such as Grand Marnier or Cointreau to the dish just before serving.

●110 calories/475 kj per portion

Plum snow

SERVES 4-6

350 g/12 oz red dessert plums,
  halved and stoned

300 ml/½ pint water
100 g/4 oz sugar
1 rounded tablespoon (1 sachet)
  powdered gelatine
3 egg whites
1-2 plums, stoned and thinly
  sliced, and crystallized rose
  petals, to decorate

1 Put 3 tablespoons of the water into a small heatproof bowl and set aside. Put the dessert plums and remaining water into a large saucepan, bring to the boil, then cover and simmer the plums gently for 15-20 minutes until they are very soft.
2 Stir in the sugar until it has dissolved, then set aside.
3 Meanwhile, sprinkle the gelatine over the reserved water and leave to soak for 5 minutes until spongy.
4 Pour the plum mixture into the goblet of a blender and blend until smooth, then pass through a sieve into a large bowl.
5 Stand the bowl of gelatine in a pan of gently simmering water and stir until the gelatine has dissolved. Then pour the gelatine into the plum purée, in a thin steady stream, whisking until it is thoroughly blended. [!]
6 Refrigerate for about 45 minutes, stirring occasionally, until mixture is thick and beginning to set. Add the egg whites and whisk until very thick and fluffy.
7 Pour into a 1.25 L/2 pint serving dish and refrigerate for about 4 hours until set.
8 Decorate with plum slices and crystallized rose petals and serve.

Cook's Notes

 TIME
About 1½ hours to make snow, including 45 minutes chilling time. Allow 4 hours for setting.

WATCHPOINT
Always add gelatine to the fruit purée and not other way around. To prevent 'threads' of hot gelatine from setting in the mixture, pour the gelatine in a thin steady stream and make sure that both the purée and the gelatine are at the same temperature.

SERVING IDEAS
Serve this light frothy pudding with small sweet biscuits or make your own plain butter biscuits and cut them into pretty heart or butterfly shapes.

●150 calories/625 kj per portion

Stuffed peaches

SERVES 4

 4 fresh peaches or 8 canned peach
halves
75g/3 oz full-fat soft cheese
3-4 tablespoons natural yoghurt
2 drops almond essence
2 teaspoons caster sugar
1 tablespoon flaked almonds

1 Skin the fresh peaches, if using (see Cook's tip), then cut the peaches in half and carefully remove the stones.

2 Blend the cheese with just enough yoghurt to give a thick, smooth mixture. Add the almond essence plus sugar to taste.

3 Spoon the mixture into the cavities of each peach half then refrigerate.

4 Toast the almonds in a moderate oven or under the grill.

5 Just before serving the peaches, sprinkle with the almonds.

Cook's Notes

 TIME
10 minutes plus at least 30 minutes for chilling.

 COOK'S TIP
To remove the skins from the peaches, dip them in boiling water for 1 minute, then peel them.

● 145 calories/625 kj per portion

Honeyed apricot whips

SERVES 4

100 g/4 oz dried apricots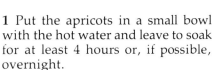
300 ml/½ pint hot water
2 tablespoons clear honey
300 g/10 oz natural yoghurt
2 egg whites
boudoir biscuits or chocolate
   fingers, to serve

1 Put the apricots in a small bowl with the hot water and leave to soak for at least 4 hours or, if possible, overnight.

2 Turn the apricots and water into a heavy-based saucepan. Add the honey, cover and simmer very gently for about 20 minutes, until the apricots are tender. Remove from the heat and leave to cool completely.

3 Purée the apricots with the cooking syrup and yoghurt in a blender. Alternatively, press the apricots through a nylon sieve, then stir in the cooking syrup and fold in the yoghurt.

4 Whisk the egg whites until they stand in soft peaks. Using a metal spoon, lightly stir 1 tablespoon of the whisked egg whites into the apricot purée mixture, then fold in the remainder.

5 Spoon the whip into stemmed glasses. Serve at once, or refrigerate until serving time. Serve with the biscuits.

Cook's Notes

TIME
1¼ hours (including cooling time), but remember that the apricots need to be soaked for a minimum of 4 hours before they are ready to be cooked.

DID YOU KNOW
Yoghurt is a high-protein, low-calorie food, and dried apricots are a good source of iron. This dessert is suitable for anyone on a low-fat diet.

●135 calories/575 kj per portion

Mango
spoon sweet

SERVES 4-6

2 ripe mangoes, total weight about 750 g/1½ lb (see Preparation)
225 g/8 oz can pineapple rings in natural juice, drained with 100 ml/3½ fl oz juice reserved
100 g/4 oz green grapes, halved and seeded
100 g/4 oz black grapes, halved and seeded

1 Put the mangoes in a blender with their juice and the measured pineapple juice. Work to a purée, then pour into a large bowl.
2 Cut each pineapple ring into 6 pieces and add to the mango purée together with the grapes. Cover and refrigerate for 30 minutes.
3 Spoon the mixture into 4-6 small dishes. Serve chilled.

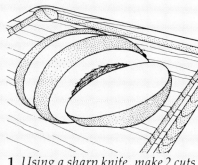
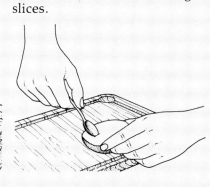

Pear wine sorbet

SERVES 4

 4 firm dessert pears, peeled, cored and sliced (see Buying guide)

☐! 150 ml/¼ pint white wine (see Buying guide)

✳ 75 g/3 oz caster sugar
strip of lemon rind
maraschino cherries, to decorate

1 Put wine, sugar and rind in a saucepan and stir over low heat until the sugar has dissolved. Bring to the boil, add the pears, then cover the pan and poach the pears gently for about 5 minutes, or until opaque. Remove the pan from the heat and set aside to cool.

2 Discard the lemon rind, reserve a few pear slices for decoration, then purée the cold mixture in a blender or press it through a sieve.

3 Pour into a freezer container, cover and freeze for several hours until firm (see Cook's tips).

4 Remove from the freezer and turn into a large bowl. ☐! Break the sorbet up with a fork, then whisk it well until slushy.

5 Spoon the mixture back into its freezer container, cover and return to the freezer for a further 3-4 hours until firm.

6 Remove the sorbet from the freezer and allow it to soften at room temperature for about 15 minutes. Then spoon it into individual glasses and serve decorated with pear slices and maraschino cherries.

Cook's Notes

TIME
Preparation takes only about 20 minutes, but remember to allow several hours for freezing time.

FREEZING
The sorbet can be stored in the freezer for up to 2 months.

BUYING GUIDE
Choose firm pears such as Conference or Comice for this sorbet. Avoid Williams which will be too soft.

It is worth choosing a good wine, or the flavour of the finished sorbet will be disappointing. Choose sweet or dry according to your taste.

WATCHPOINT
If the sorbet is too firm to mash, let it soften slightly at room temperature.

COOK'S TIPS
To make the sorbet in the freezing compart- ment of an ordinary refrige- rator, use a pre-chilled shallow metal tray for freezing the sorbet and turn the refrigerator down to its coldest setting at least 1 hour before you start making the sorbet. This will help speed up the freezing process.

VARIATION
Decorate the sorbet with a few sprigs of fresh mint in season.

● 140 calories/575 kj per portion